D1469796

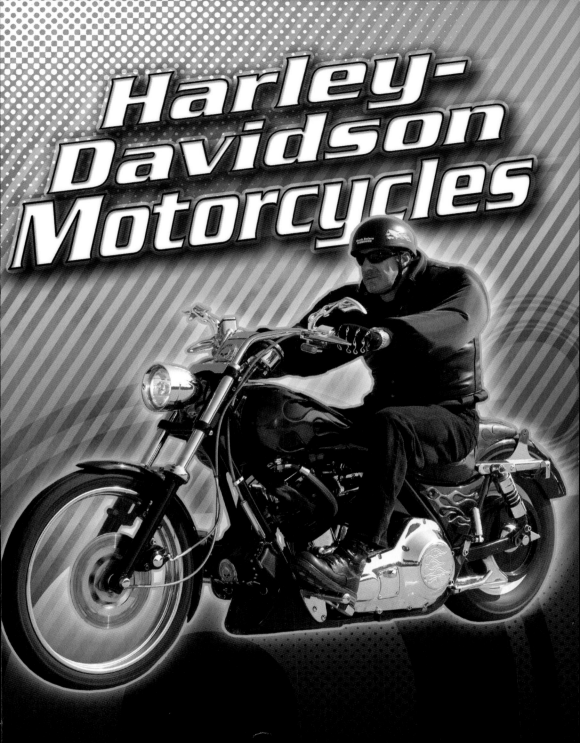

Harley-Davidson Motorcycles

BY JACK DAVID

BELLWETHER MEDIA · MINNEAPOLIS, MN

TM

Are you ready to take it to the extreme?
Torque books thrust you into the action-packed
world of sports, vehicles, and adventure. These books
may include dirt, smoke, fire, and dangerous stunts.
WARNING: read at your own risk.

Library of Congress Cataloging-in-Publication Data

David, Jack, 1968-
  Harley-Davidson motorcycles / by Jack David.
      p. cm. -- (Torque : Motorcycles)
  Includes bibliographical references and index.
  ISBN-13: 978-1-60014-134-8 (hbk. : alk. paper)
  ISBN-10: 1-60014-134-X (hbk. : alk. paper)
  1. Harley-Davidson motorcycle--Juvenile literature. 2. Motorcycles--Juvenile literature. I.
Title.

  TL448.H3D33 2008
  629.227'5--dc22
                                                                        2007014198

This edition first published in 2008 by Bellwether Media.

No part of this publication may be reproduced in whole or in part without written permission of
the publisher. For information regarding permission, write to Bellwether Media Inc., Attention:
Permissions Department, Post Office Box 1C, Minnetonka, MN 55345-9998.

Text copyright © 2008 by Bellwether Media.
SCHOLASTIC, CHILDREN'S PRESS, and associated logos are trademarks and/or registered
trademarks of Scholastic Inc. Printed in the United States of America.

CONTENTS

HARLEY-DAVIDSONS IN ACTION

A Harley-Davidson motorcycle rumbles along the mountain highway. The rider plans to meet a group of Harley riders once he passes through the mountains.

FAST FACT

THE AVERAGE COST FOR A NEW HARLEY-DAVIDSON IS ABOUT $15,000.
RARE AND COLLECTIBLE MODELS CAN COST $50,000 OR MORE.

They are heading to a **motorcycle rally** on the West Coast. The riders take pride in their American-made motorcycles. They can't wait to show them off to other Harley owners at the rally.

WHAT IS A HARLEY-DAVIDSON?

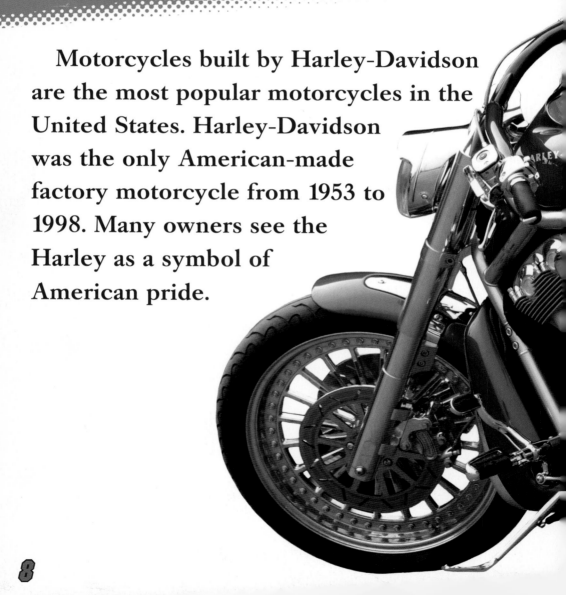

Motorcycles built by Harley-Davidson are the most popular motorcycles in the United States. Harley-Davidson was the only American-made factory motorcycle from 1953 to 1998. Many owners see the Harley as a symbol of American pride.

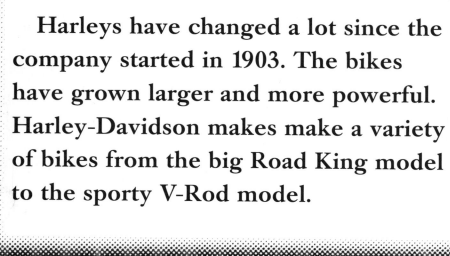

Harleys have changed a lot since the company started in 1903. The bikes have grown larger and more powerful. Harley-Davidson makes make a variety of bikes from the big Road King model to the sporty V-Rod model.

FEATURES

Most Harley-Davidsons share a few common features. Harleys are bulky bikes with low seats. They are built for comfort. They are too big for racing. The engine and other metal parts are covered with shiny **chrome** on many models. All of these features together give a Harley its famous look.

FAST FACT

MANY OWNERS ADD PARTS TO PUSH A HARLEY'S FRONT WHEEL FORWARD. THEY CALL THESE BIKES "CHOPPERS." CHOPPER RIDERS THINK THIS GIVES THEIR BIKE A TOUGHER LOOK.

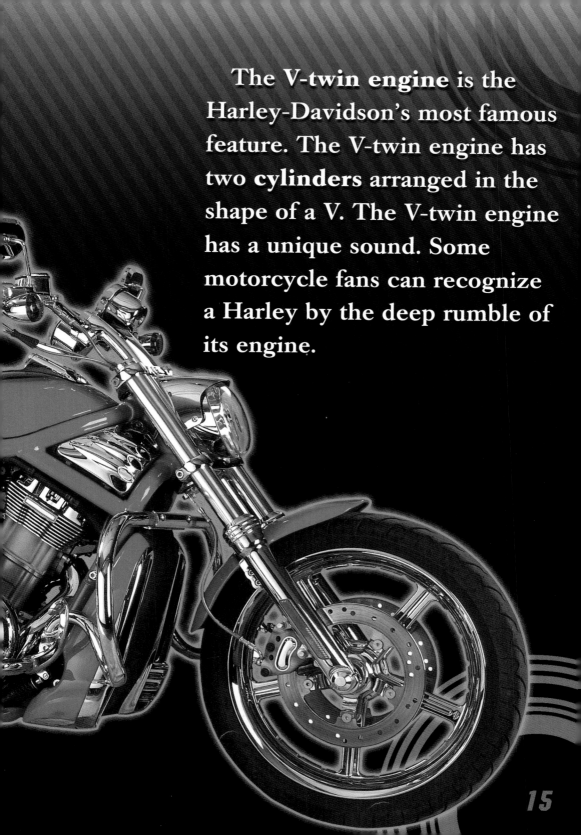

The V-twin **engine** is the Harley-Davidson's most famous feature. The V-twin engine has two **cylinders** arranged in the shape of a V. The V-twin engine has a unique sound. Some motorcycle fans can recognize a Harley by the deep rumble of its engine.

Many owners **customize** their Harleys. They change them to suit their needs. They may add a bigger engine for more power. Some owners give their bikes unique paint jobs.

Owners may add or remove parts. These owners often gather at motorcycle rallies to display their creations. Others are happy to show off their bikes by riding them through town.

19

FAST FACT

THE STURGIS MOTORCYCLE RALLY IN SOUTH DAKOTA IS THE MOST POPULAR MOTORCYCLE RALLY IN THE WORLD. AS MANY AS 500,000 RIDERS ATTEND THE EVENT EACH SUMMER.

Harley-Davidson motorcycles have been an American tradition for more than 100 years. Their comfortable ride, powerful engines, and classic design make them stand out from the crowd.

GLOSSARY

chrome–a metallic substance called chromium that gives metal objects a shiny look

customize–to modify a vehicle to suit one's individual needs

cylinder–the engine part in which fuel is burned to create power

motorcycle rally–a gathering of motorcycle riders

v-twin engine–a type of motorcycle engine with two cylinders arranged in the shape of a V

TO LEARN MORE

AT THE LIBRARY

David, Jack. *Choppers*. Minneapolis, Minn.: Bellwether, 2007.

Hill, Lee Sullivan. *Motorcycles*. Minneapolis, Minn.: Lerner Publications Co., 2004.

Schuette, Sarah L. *Harley-Davidson Motorcycles*. Mankato, Minn.: Capstone Press, 2007.

ON THE WEB

Learning more about motorcycles is as easy as 1, 2, 3.

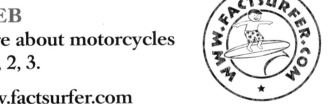

1. Go to www.factsurfer.com

2. Enter "motorcycles" into search box.

3. Click the "Surf" button and you will see a list of related web sites.

With factsurfer.com, finding more information is just a click away.

INDEX

The photographs in this book are reproduced through the courtesy of: AFP/Getty Images, front cover, pp. 6, 11, 17, 18-19; Ethan Mill/Getty Images, pp. 4-5; Alan Stone/Alamy, pp. 8-9, 14 (top); Juan Martinez, pp. 10-11, 12-13, 14-15; SuperStock/agefotostock, pp. 20-21.